D1707861

TABLE OF CONTENTS

Octopuses

The octopus is one of the most remarkable animals of the seas. It can change color and shape. It can swim by jet propulsion. It can probably see very well, and it can confuse enemies with a "smoke screen" of ink. Perhaps most remarkable, an octopus seems quite intelligent by human measure.

An octopus can crawl over the ocean bottom or jet through the water.

Octopuses are **invertebrates**. Invertebrates are animals without backbones, such as insects, worms, spiders, sea stars, jellyfish, and clams. Most invertebrates don't have brains.

An octopus out and about can find its way home.

But the octopus is a most unusual invertebrate. It has a large and **complex** brain. That provides the octopus with the ability to learn and remember certain things.

Among invertebrate animals, the octopus may be a genius!

The squid is a close cousin of the octopus.

Among the thousands of kinds of invertebrates, octopuses belong to the mollusks. Clams, oysters, and mussels are common mollusks.

Within the mollusk group, octopuses are most closely related to squid, nautiluses, and cuttlefish. Scientists call these animals **cephalopods**.

What Octopuses Look Like

The octopus has a soft, rounded body with two large eyes. Scientists have identified about 100 **species** of octopuses. The largest is the giant octopus of the Pacific Ocean. It can weigh more than 110 pounds (50 kilograms).

The soft, flexible octopus can squeeze into tight spaces.

Octopus eyes probably provide unusually good vision.

Octopuses range from less than 1 inch (2 centimeters) to more than 20 feet (6 meters) in length. That includes the length of their eight **tentacles**. The tentacles reach out from the animal's head.

The main part of an octopus body is covered by a fleshy covering called a mantle. An octopus flexes the mantle to force water from its body through a tube. The force propels the octopus through the water.

By forcing water with its mantle through a body tube, an octopus swims by jet propulsion.

Octopus tentacles are equipped with little suckers. Suckers allow an octopus to grip its **prey** or any hard surface tightly. The suckers are extremely sensitive to touch.

DID YOU KNOW?

Octopuses are generally reddish brown. They can change color to suit their surroundings.

The suckers on octopus tentacles have great holding power.

Where Octopuses Live

Octopuses live in shallow and deep seas throughout the world. Most species live on the ocean floor. Some species choose rocky areas. Others like sandy or muddy bottoms.

Some live hidden in shelters they build of rocks. Some find ready-made homes, such as empty bottles.

An octopus hides on a coral reef by matching the reef colors.

Hiding in an empty shell, an octopus prepares to eat a snail.

Predator and Prey

As **predators**, octopuses eat live prey, including crabs, lobsters, worms, fish, and other mollusks.

Sometimes an octopus swims to find prey. At other times, an octopus waits patiently for prey to swim by its den.

An octopus grabs prey with its tentacles. The tentacles transport it to the octopus's beak-like jaws. The octopus bites the prey and injects **venom**. The venom weakens and kills prey, which the octopus then begins to eat.

DID YOU KNOW?

Octopuses are themselves prey for certain seals, whales, fish, and sea turtles.

An octopus finishes its meal of tuna crab, nearly hidden by the mantle.

The Life Cycle of Octopuses

Depending on the species, a female octopus lays from 150 to 400,000 eggs. Some octopus species hatch looking like tiny adults. Others are far less developed as babies.

Among some species, the female octopus guards her eggs for more than a year. During that time the females waste away. Many female octopus species die about the time their eggs hatch.

A female octopus surrounds herself with eggs.

Octopuses and People

Octopuses are not considered dangerous to people. They can bite, of course, but only when handled or cornered. Stories of giant octopuses capturing and drowning people are not based on facts.

In some countries, such as Japan, octopuses are caught for food. In North America, octopuses are more popular for studies of their behavior than for food.

A diver swims with a giant octopus in the Pacific Ocean.

Glossary

cephalopods (SEF uh luh PODZ) — a group of invertebrate animals including squids, octopuses, cuttlefishes, and chambered nautiluses

complex (kom PLEKS) — complicated; of many parts; the opposite of simple

invertebrates (IN VERT uh BRAYTZ) — animals without backbones

predators (PRED uh turz) — animals that hunt other animals for food

prey (PRAY) — any animal caught and eaten by another animal

species (SPEE sheez) — one kind of animal within a group of closely related animals, such as a *giant Pacific* octopus

tentacles (TENT uh kulz) — long, flexible "fingers" or "arms" reaching from the heads or mouths of certain animals and used for such purposes as grabbing prey

venom (VEN um) — a poison produced by certain animals for defense or to kill prey

Index

Further Reading

Hirschmann, Kris. *Octopus.* Thomson Gale, 2002
Swanson, Diane. *Octopuses.* Gareth Stevens Audio, 2002

Websites To Visit

www.marinelab.sarasota.fl.us/OCTOPI.HTM
www.enchantedlearning.com/subjects/invertebrates/octopus/Octopuscoloring.shtml/

About The Author

Lynn M. Stone is the author and photographer of many children's books. Lynn is a former teacher who travels worldwide to pursue his varied interests.